First-time Visitors

Written by Jenny Feely

Flying Start
to Literacy®

Contents

Introduction

Two men had been climbing the mountain for more than a day. It was freezing cold and now it looked like they could go no further. A nearly vertical icy cliff stood between the men and their dream of being the first people to reach the summit of the highest mountain on Earth.

One of the men slowly climbed up the cliff. If he fell, there were no ropes to save him. At last, he reached the top of the icy cliff. He threw a rope down to the other man. Together, they climbed up to the top of the mountain. They were the first people to get there.

Why were these men doing this? Why were they willing to take such risks? The answer is simple. They wanted to be the first to visit the highest place on Earth.

It was the same for the first people to reach the South
Pole. They trekked through snow, ice and blizzards for
months. Eventually, one team succeeded. But another
didn't – in the freezing conditions and without food, all
in this second team perished.

These people were all driven by the quest to find out about the unknown. The quest for knowledge and scientific information has inspired people to invent machines that have enabled them to travel up into the atmosphere and out into space. They had to defy gravity and survive in an uninhabitable environment that lacked oxygen.

Throughout history, people have dreamt of being the first to visit places on Earth and beyond. Often these were places that few people believed could ever be reached. They all had to overcome unknown obstacles and challenges in their pursuit of knowledge, scientific information and adventure. And they wanted to be the first.

First to the South Pole

The South Pole is in Antarctica and is the southern-most place on Earth. Even today, travelling in Antarctica is difficult and dangerous, and no one lives there all the time. It is extremely cold and covered in snow and ice all year long.

In 1911, two men, Roald Amundsen from Norway and the British explorer Robert Falcon Scott, had the same dream: to be the first to lead a successful expedition to the South Pole.

At that time, not much was known about Antarctica and there were no maps. The South Pole was more than 1200 kilometres from the Antarctic coast. There was no way to communicate with others and no information about the weather. The extreme cold conditions are life threatening.

But these challenges did not stop Amundsen and Scott. They arrived in Antarctica in January 1911. Both teams set up base camps and began to prepare their routes by taking supplies inland to be used on the return journey.

Both expeditions chose different routes to take, and different ways to travel and to carry their equipment and food. These decisions influenced how the race ended.

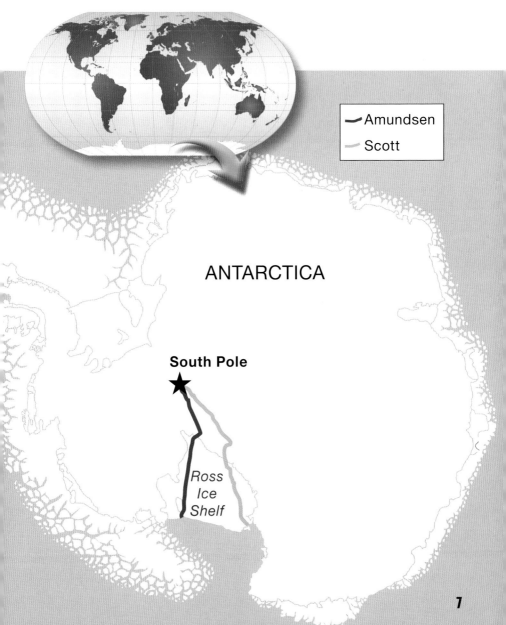

Roald Amundsen

Amundsen had lived with the Inuit people in the Arctic. From them, he had learnt that dog sleds and fur-lined clothes worked well in polar conditions. He chose these for the expedition.

On 20 October 1911, Amundsen set off for the South Pole with five men, who were all experienced polar explorers. Their expedition had four sleds and 52 dogs.

The first part of their journey across the flat Ross Ice Shelf was the least difficult. Then, they had to climb up a 50-kilometre-long icy glacier to reach the Antarctic plateau. Amundsen commented in his journal:

> In the mist and driving snow it looked as if we had a frozen lake before us, but it proved to be a sloping plateau of ice, full of small blocks of ice ... First, a man fell through, then a couple of dogs, but they got up again all right. We could not, of course, use our skis on this smooth-polished ice, but we got on fairly well with the sleds.

On 14 December 1911, Amundsen and his team arrived at the South Pole. He had won the race.

Amundsen and his team on dog sleds

The return journey was quick. On 18 December they left the South Pole and arrived at base camp 39 days later.

Amundsen's route was 60 kilometres shorter than Scott's route. They had much better weather than Scott, and the route they chose was easier to navigate.

Amundsen's Journey

14 January 1911	20 October 1911	14 December 1911	18 December 1911	26 January 1912
Arrives in Antarctica	Sets off for South Pole	Reaches South Pole	Starts return journey	Returns to ship

Robert Falcon Scott

Scott's expedition of 16 men set out for the South Pole on 1 November 1911. As well as dogs, they used ponies and motorised sleds to carry supplies. In the extreme cold, the ponies soon died and the motor sleds did not work, so they had to pull the sleds themselves. Also, their clothing was not warm enough and Scott and his men were constantly cold.

Scott and three others finally reached the South Pole on 17 January 1912 – 33 days after Amundsen. Badly weakened by the lack of food and exhaustion, they set off on the return journey to base camp. They had to pull their sleds the 1200 kilometres. Only 18 kilometres from camp, all members of the Scott expedition died.

The last entry in Scott's diary records the tragedy:

Thursday, March 29th – Since the 21st we have had a continuous gale ... Every day we have been ready to start for our depot 18 kilometres away, but outside the door of the tent it remains a scene of whirling drift. I do not think we can hope for any better things now. We shall stick it out to the end, but we are getting weaker, of course, and the end cannot be far. It seems a pity, but I do not think I can write more. R. Scott.

Scott and his men at the South Pole. There they discovered the Norwegian flag, which meant that Amundsen's team had beaten them.

Scott's Journey

5 January 1911	1 November 1911	11 December 1911	1 January 1912	17 January 1912	29 March 1912
Sets up camp in Antarctica	Sets off for South Pole	All dogs and ponies have died; men have to pull the sleds	Reaches the Antarctic plateau	Reaches South Pole	Scott writes last entry in diary

Chapter 2

First to the top

Mount Everest is the highest mountain in the world. This rugged mountain is often called the "unclimbable mountain" because of its steep slopes that are covered in glaciers and ice. It is always extremely cold on the mountain and low temperatures can cause hypothermia and frostbite. The lack of oxygen near the top of the mountain can cause altitude sickness.

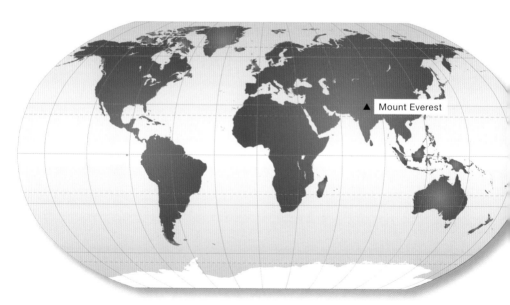

▲ Mount Everest

Mount Everest is located in the Himalayan mountain range on the border between Nepal and Tibet.

The weather is unpredictable. A bright sunny day can suddenly become a blizzard-filled nightmare with fierce winds. Without warning, snow and ice can form avalanches that crash down the mountain.

The first attempt to climb Mount Everest, which was unsuccessful, was made in 1921. Over the next 30 years many people tried, and failed, to climb to the top of the mountain, which is called the summit. As people climbed higher up the mountain, they collected information that helped future expeditions to have a better chance of success.

Altitude sickness

The summit of Mount Everest is 8848 metres high. There is not much oxygen in the air near the top of the mountain. This makes it hard for climbers to breathe. It can also cause dizziness, nausea and bad headaches. Climbers spend a lot of their time slowly getting their bodies used to increasingly high altitudes. This is why it can take climbers many weeks to climb Mount Everest.

A huge expedition

In 1953, British mountaineer John Hunt led a large expedition to climb Mount Everest. Of the 400 members, more than 360 of them were porters who carried 4535 kilograms of supplies. The porters were local Sherpa people from the mountains of the Himalayas in Nepal. They were used to the conditions on the mountains and dealing with the weather. Many Sherpas are also skilled and experienced mountain guides and climbers, and their knowledge of the mountain was vital to an expedition's success.

Sherpas weigh baggage before it is divided up to be carried on the 1953 expedition.

People who attempt to climb to the summit of Mount Everest have to carry tanks of oxygen because there is not enough oxygen in the air to breathe.

Ten members of the expedition were mountain climbers, including Sherpa Tenzing Norgay who was an experienced mountain guide with a great ambition to climb Mount Everest. He had been on six previous expeditions and had climbed further up Mount Everest than anyone else.

After months of planning and organising, the expedition began to climb. Two months later, they were ready to attempt the summit. Hunt chose two teams of climbers for the final ascent. Each team had two climbers.

The first team climbed to about 90 metres short of the summit, the highest anyone had yet reached, but they were forced to turn back after bad weather set in and because they were running low on oxygen in their tanks.

Reaching the summit

On 28 May, the second team, Edmund Hillary from New Zealand and Tenzing Norgay, got the opportunity to climb. On the first day, they climbed to 8500 metres, where they pitched their tents for the night.

The next day, the climb went well, until they came to a 12-metre-high rock face. Slowly, Hillary pushed himself up a crack in the rock face. At the top, he lowered a rope for Norgay to climb up. Together, they continued along the ridge that led to the summit.

On 29 May 1953, Hillary and Norgay stepped onto the summit and became the first people to ever set foot on the top of Mount Everest.

When they returned from the mountain, reporters wanted to know who had been the first to set foot on the top. They told the reporters:

To a mountaineer, it's of no great consequence who actually sets foot first.

It wasn't until many years later that Norgay revealed that it was Hillary who had stepped onto the summit first.

Tenzing Norgay (left) and Edmund Hillary

Since the first successful expedition, thousands of people have climbed Mount Everest. It is still a difficult and dangerous place to climb, but the first people to visit the top of the world's highest mountain showed others that it could be done.

Frozen shoes

One day, Hillary woke up to find that his boots had frozen solid outside his tent. It took him two hours to warm them up so that he could wear them on the final ascent.

Chapter 3

First to the stratosphere

Members of the Piccard family from Switzerland have set many first-time records. They have been the first to the stratosphere and the first to the bottom of the ocean. The first member of the family to go where no one had gone before was the scientist Auguste Piccard. In 1931, he was the first person to travel to the upper part of the atmosphere, which is called the stratosphere.

The Piccard family in 1931: Auguste (second from right) was the first person to travel to the stratosphere; his son Jacques (third from the left) was the first person to reach the deepest part of the ocean.

To travel up into the atmosphere and beyond is difficult and dangerous. This is because there is less oxygen in the upper atmosphere. In order for people to travel away from Earth and high up into the atmosphere, they need to have enough oxygen to breathe. They also need to find a way to escape the Earth's gravity. Gravity is the force that pulls everything towards Earth.

The balloon carrying Auguste Piccard towards the stratosphere

Light and airtight

To survive the journey, Piccard invented and built a capsule that was airtight so he and his assistant, Paul Kipfer, would have oxygen to breathe. He designed the capsule so that it was light enough to be lifted into the atmosphere by a large balloon filled with helium, which is lighter than air.

Auguste Piccard and Paul Kipfer in 1931. They wear special helmets to prevent head injuries in the balloon.

The balloon took them as high as 16 kilometres above the surface of Earth. No one had been that high before. They had a view of Earth that no one had ever seen before. And they saw the edge of space – a deep, dark blue.

The scene of the crash landing in Austria

But when they decided to return to Earth they couldn't make the balloon descend. Their oxygen was running out and if they couldn't get back to the surface of the Earth they would surely die. Then, in the cool evening air, the helium in the balloon started to shrink and the balloon began to sink back to Earth. Finally, it crash-landed on a glacier in Austria, where they were rescued.

Piccard's invention of an air-tight capsule enabled further exploration of the atmosphere. The flight proved that people could travel through the atmosphere and that, in future, they would travel into space.

Chapter 4

First to the bottom of the ocean

Reaching the deepest part of the ocean was once thought to be an impossible task. Travelling underwater is difficult. There is no air to breathe. As the ocean gets deeper and deeper, there is less light and it gets colder and colder. The weight of the water gets very heavy and the pressure is high. In the deepest places in the ocean, the pressure is so great that it would crush most submarines. The deepest place in the ocean is in the Mariana Trench in the Pacific Ocean.

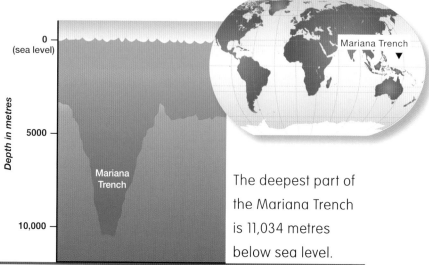

The deepest part of the Mariana Trench is 11,034 metres below sea level.

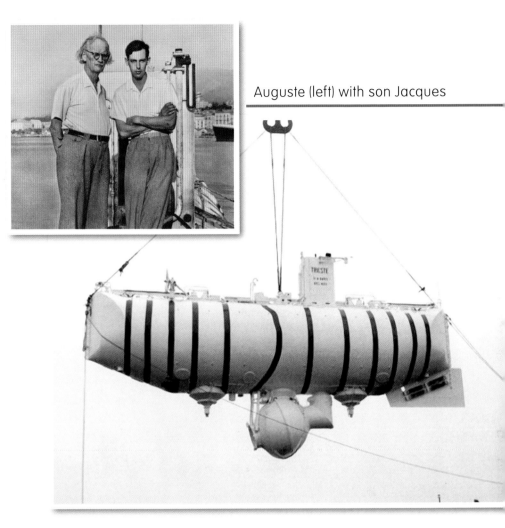

Auguste (left) with son Jacques

The Piccard's bathyscaphe, the *Trieste*

Using knowledge gained from the airtight capsule flight, Auguste Piccard worked with his son Jacques to invent the first deep-sea diving vessel, a bathyscaphe called the *Trieste*. On 23 January 1960, Jacques Piccard and Don Walsh were the first people to dive down to the Mariana Trench. Their journey took four hours and 45 minutes.

As the *Trieste* descended, the sea became darker and darker. The *Trieste* creaked as the water pressure increased. Then one of the windows cracked and the vessel shook. Piccard and Walsh feared that the bathyscaphe would not survive the crushing pressure. Would the window break? Would the sea come rushing in? They continued the descent and safely reached the deepest place in the ocean. They spent about 20 minutes at the bottom of the ocean. The lights on the exterior of the bathyscaphe lit up the ocean floor and they saw fish no one had seen before.

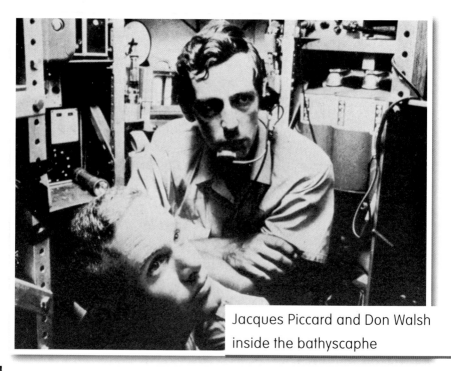

Jacques Piccard and Don Walsh inside the bathyscaphe

More firsts for the Piccard family

Bertrand Piccard is a member of the record-breaking Piccard family. Like his grandfather Auguste and father Jacques, Bertrand loves inventing and exploring.

In 1999, Bertrand made the first non-stop balloon flight around the world. In 2016, Bertrand and co-pilot André Borschberg made the first round-the-world flight on a plane powered only by the sun. Their 40,233-kilometre journey was the first time that people had flown around the Earth without using fuel.

Bertrand Piccard and co-pilot André Borschberg made the first solar-powered flight in this plane.

Chapter 5

First to space and beyond

Beyond the Earth's atmosphere is space. There is no air, water or food in space and it is freezing cold. Space explorers have to take everything they need with them. For space travellers, coming back to Earth is very dangerous. The Earth's gravity pulls spacecraft towards the Earth at great speeds and the atmosphere causes the spacecraft to heat up dangerously. But, despite all of these challenges, people have travelled into space.

The space race

The effort to reach space became a race between two countries: the United States and Russia. Both wanted to be first and spent huge amounts of money to achieve this aim.

The first person to travel beyond the Earth's atmosphere was the Russian cosmonaut Yuri Gagarin. He completed this record-breaking journey on 12 April 1960. On this trip, Gagarin completed the first orbit of the Earth by a human and was able to view the Earth from space.

Living without gravity

Gagarin was the first person to experience what it was like to be away from the Earth's gravity. He described it as feeling like he was "suspended".

Stepping onto the moon

Having successfully visited space, the next challenge was to be first to step onto the surface of the moon. It was a huge challenge. How would explorers live in space for long enough to reach the moon? How would they land on the moon? What would it be like on the moon?

The United States and Russia launched more and more rockets taking people further from the Earth, collecting information about space and what it was like to live there. Each space mission tested new equipment. Each mission got people closer and closer to stepping onto the moon. Then, on 20 July 1969, the first spacecraft, the *Eagle*, landed on the moon and astronauts Neil Armstrong and Edwin "Buzz" Aldrin stepped onto its surface – the first people ever to do so. Armstrong was the first out of the *Eagle* and as his foot settled into the moon dust he said:

"That's one small step for a man, one giant leap for mankind."

Aldrin and the US flag on the moon

Armstrong and Aldrin explored the moon for three hours, conducting experiments to learn about the surface of the moon and also about the solar wind. They collected things such as dirt and rocks to bring back to Earth to be studied. They put a United States flag on the moon and left a sign that said:

"Here men from the planet Earth first set foot upon the moon July 1969, AD. We came in peace for all mankind."

29

Conclusion

The journeys of first-time visitors have made it possible for others to follow in their footsteps. People continue to explore ways to visit the places that no one has ever been to before. They look to the planets and beyond. Being the first to go there is their dream.

Who will be the next first-time visitor? Where will they go and how will they get there? Will they come back to tell us about what they saw? Only time will tell.

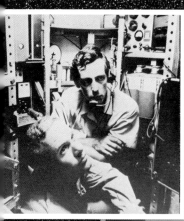

Glossary

bathyscaphe a deep-sea diving boat that travels underwater

frostbite a condition in which part of your body (such as your fingers or toes) freezes or almost freezes

hypothermia a condition in which the temperature of your body is very low

motorised having a motor that produces power for doing work

solar winds a type of wind that travels from the sun through the solar system

space mission a journey into space for a specific reason